Getting a Result

GW00597463

Iain Maitland is a Lecturer in Supervisory Management at Otley College, near Ipswich, and the author of over 20 books such as *How to Recruit* and *The Barclays Guide to Managing Staff for the Small Business*. Before becoming a lecturer and author, he owned and ran numerous small businesses in the retail sector.

To Tracey, Michael and Sophie

Other titles in this series

Choosing the Players by Penny Hackett
Keeping the Team in Shape by John McManus

We are grateful to the National Federation of Self Employed and Small Businesses Ltd for their help and cooperation in the preparation of this series.

The Institute of Personnel and Development is the leading publisher of books and reports for personnel and training professionals and students and for all those concerned with the effective management and development of people at work. For full details of all our titles please telephone the Publishing Department on 081 946 9100.

Managing People in the Small and Growing Business

Getting a Result

Iain Maitland

Cartoons by Katherine Bowry

Institute of Personnel and Development

Typesetting by The Comp-Room, Aylesbury
and printed in Great Britain by
the Cromwell Press, Wiltshire

British Library Cataloguing-in-Publication Data
A catalogue record for this book is available from the
British Library

The views expressed in this book are the author's own and
may not necessarily reflect those of the IPD.

**INSTITUTE OF PERSONNEL
AND DEVELOPMENT**

IPD House, Camp Road, London SW19 4UX
Tel: 081 946 9100   Fax: 081 947 2570
Registered office as above. Registered Charity No. 1038333
A company limited by guarantee. Registered in England No. 2931892

Contents

v

Preface

Getting a Result is written for you – the owner or manager of a small but growing business. Perhaps you are a retailer who wants to know how to train staff properly, or an office manager seeking to provide a working environment which will improve work-rate and performance. Possibly, you own a warehouse and want to find out what you can do to make boring and mundane jobs more interesting, or manage a factory and wish to devise a pay scheme to motivate employees. This book tells you how to do this, and much more.

'You and Your Staff' asks how you can get the best from your employees and looks at identifying your expectations, recognising staff needs and devising an action plan for success. 'Staff Development' explains this key topic by outlining how to install, train and assess employees properly. 'Working Conditions' considers the significance of the workplace and goes on to investigate setting minimum standards, making improvements and maintaining a healthy and safe environment. 'Job Enjoyment' explores the importance of this major issue and discusses matching employees and employment, job improvement techniques and redesigning jobs to suit staff. 'Pay and Benefits' contemplates whether employees are motivated only by pay and examines pay levels, pay systems and other financial benefits which form part of the overall pay package. 'Employer–Employee Relations' queries the relevance of relationships and details how to be a good leader, communicate with each other and build a first-rate team. Chapter summaries and a 'Useful Addresses' section complete the text.

Whether you own or manage a shop, office, warehouse, factory, hotel, restaurant or any other type of concern, this book will be of interest to you. Written by an author who has run several small businesses over many years and is aware of the wants and needs of such firms and their employees, the text addresses those topics of key importance to you. All in all, this is a valuable, hands-on guide to making the most of your staff, now and in the future.

Iain Maitland

1 You and Your Staff

Small business owners and managers have to make the most of their staff if they are to be successful. This chapter considers:

- getting the best from your employees
- identifying your expectations
- recognising staff needs
- devising an action plan.

How do you get the best from your employees?

Getting the best from your staff need not be a time-consuming or costly task, as long as it is approached on a clear and logical, step-by-step basis. To begin with, you have to identify your expectations, setting down a list of what you want from your employees, which may include anything from turning up for work on time to fitting into your team. Next, you must recognise your staff's needs – which may be very different from what you

1

Identify your expectations

first imagine them to be. Then, you have to devise an action plan, scheduling the changes and developments that will fulfil both staff needs and your expectations, *and* enable you to make the most of your employees. All without taking up too much time or money.

Identifying your expectations

First things first – you must sit down and work out precisely what it is that you expect from your staff. This should be a relatively straightforward matter and you will probably make a note of such matters as turning up for work each and every day, arriving on time, taking the agreed coffee-, lunch- and tea-breaks and no more, and going home at the set time, but no earlier. You can possibly think of a whole host of other practicalities that staff should adhere to, ranging from following your particular rules and procedures to carrying out work practices in a safety-conscious manner. Much will depend on the type of small firm you run.

After that, you may consider each individual employee in turn, and what you want from them. You might add notes to your list about appearance, speech and general conduct, that they should fit easily into the team, communicating and getting on well with you and their colleagues. In all probability, other personal features will come into your mind, too, that you feel should be incorporated into your lengthening list, anything from being helpful, through self-discipline, to loyalty. It is up to you.

It is likely that most of your expectations will focus upon staff work-rate, performance and adaptability. You will expect them to know their jobs well, be confident enough to do them on their own with minimal fuss, and with any problems and difficulties being resolved promptly and efficiently. In addition, you will

3

want them to work as hard as they can, and to the best of their abilities, so that the quantity *and* quality of their work is as high as possible. Contemplate any other expectations that you wish to include as well – potentially, this is almost an endless list!

Recognising staff needs

You must follow this detailed examination of your expectations by considering your employees' needs. What is it that they want from your firm? 'Nothing but money, and lots of it,' may be your immediate response, but this is rarely true in practice. Of course, money is as important to your staff as it is to everyone else, but usually they have other, different needs as well, some of which are of greater significance to them than money alone. After all, your employees will realise that cash is especially tight in smaller concerns, which are used to operating on limited sales and profit margins. Talk to your employees, asking them about themselves and their requirements, to discover what they really want. You may be surprised by their comments.

Most staff will wish to enjoy a good, communicative relationship with you and their other colleagues in the workplace. Typically, they will want you to be friendly, pleasant and interested in them, respecting and trusting them to carry out their work, and helping them to settle any problems and difficulties in an efficient and effective manner. Similarly, they may also wish to have an equally comfortable relationship with fellow employees, looking to them for help and support as and when required. They will probably want to feel they are valued and liked members of a team.

The majority of your employees will wish to know what they are supposed to be doing and feel capable of performing the job properly. Not surprisingly, they will also want to enjoy it, and perhaps feel a sense of status and achievement. Likewise, many staff will want to ensure that they receive a fair and acceptable pay package, comprising a good level of pay and any associated fringe benefits that a small business is able to afford. They will wish to work in a healthy and pleasant environment as well.

They will all have different requirements in terms of their work. Some want an easy job, others a difficult and demanding one. Furthermore, employees' requirements can change from time to time. As an example, those staff who enjoy a challenging job may occasionally wish to do easier tasks and duties, perhaps because they feel ill or have a heavy workload that day. You need to appreciate that everyone is unique, treating them as individuals as well as a team. All you can state with any certainty is that you have to satisfy and motivate each and every one of them to avoid absences, lateness, poor work-rate and performance, resignations and dismissals. Keep them happy, to get them going.

Devising an action plan

So, you know what to expect from your staff, and have a better idea of what your employees want from you, colleagues, the job and the firm. You now need to work out the changes and developments that should be introduced so that both you and your staff obtain what you want from each other. Most if not all of them can probably be grouped under various, common headings – staff development, working conditions, job enjoyment, pay and benefits and employer – employee relations.

You will appreciate that staff need to be developed to the best of their abilities, typically through installing them properly into the business, training them to make the most of their skills, knowledge and experience, and assessing them regularly to ensure they are satisfied and doing well. Working conditions are important, too, and may have to be improved to make them healthy and safe. Particular thought might need to be given to such areas as layout and space, heating and ventilation, light and noise, social areas, equipment and machinery, and accidents and emergencies – all of which can have adverse effects on employees if they are unsatisfactory.

Obviously, the tasks and duties that staff perform are of crucial significance – everyone wants to have job enjoyment, and will probably work harder and better if they do. Thus, you might want to see that employees and their employment are well matched, improving and perhaps redesigning jobs or the conditions of their work area as and when required. The pay and benefits received by staff may have to be reviewed, with attention being given to pay levels and other, affordable fringe benefits available to them. You may decide to make some amendments or additions to the overall pay package provided.

Possibly, your examination of your own expectations and staff requirements may have indicated that your employer–employee relationship is not quite as strong as it could be, and you may wish to take steps to remedy matters in this area. Perhaps you want to change your approach to become a good leader, adjust your communication methods to communicate better with each other, or simply wish to do what is needed to build up a first-rate team.

Any planned activities will need to be contemplated carefully before implementation so that you can appraise their advantages, disadvantages, costs and likely benefits for you, the small business owner or manager who may be short of time and money. Do the pros of assessing staff outweigh the cons? What are the time and financial costs involved in providing an agreeable pay package? How will the firm gain from improved communications and team spirit? These and many other questions have to be asked, and answered positively, before you can go on to bring in changes that will help you to make the most of your team.

Summary

- Getting the best from staff involves identifying the employer's expectations, recognising employees' needs and devising an action plan to implement changes and developments which will satisfy both parties.
- An employer's expectations of staff will vary according to individual circumstances but are most likely to focus upon work-rate and performance. Potentially, the list of expectations is never-ending.
- Employees' needs are all different, and tend to be many and varied. Money is rarely the only requirement, although it is usually significant.
- An action plan will be unique to a particular situation but will probably incorporate the key topics of staff development, working conditions, job enjoyment, pay and benefits and employer–employee relations in one way or another.

2   Staff Development

 The owners and managers of small firms should be aware of the importance of staff development with regard to making the most of their team. In this chapter, we look at:

- what staff development is
- installing employees
- training staff
- assessing employees.

What is staff development?

'Staff development' may be defined quite simply as 'the systematic and continual process of developing effective employees to meet the requirements of a business organisation'. In order to achieve this, you have to approach staff development in a clear and logical manner – installing employees properly on a planned, step-by-step basis, identifying their training needs, studying training methods, deciding on an appropriate training programme and evaluating training to judge its effects. Also, it is wise to assess employees regularly to make certain they are developing in an effective and efficient manner. If not, perhaps more or different training procedures are required.

Installing employees

The process of installing a new employee – more formally known as 'induction' – is as relevant to a smaller concern as it is to a larger one, with its own personnel department, induction courses and other, elaborate activities. It serves several purposes, each of which should help you to get the best from that recruit, now *and* in the future. If arranged carefully and successfully, it should educate the employee about all aspects of the job and firm, highlight any problems or difficulties which need to be resolved promptly, give him or her the confidence to do the job well and ensure he or she fits into the team in a smooth and effective manner.

Of course, if you own or run a small business, you may feel that your time and that of your existing staff is fully occupied and you do not have the resources to spend on settling in a recruit. Perhaps you are inclined to adopt a 'sink or swim' policy – here's the job, get on with it! This is an understandable instinct, but can be seen to be a short-sighted approach on further reflection. Not knowing what to do, he or she will make more mistakes at work, have to keep asking you questions about the job, procedures, the firm and so on, all of which means extra money and time spent on that person in the long term. For a smaller concern, induction can be kept relatively simple and straightforward, and viewed in various stages – on acceptance of the job offer, on induction day, and the first day, week and month at work.

On acceptance

Your induction of a new employee should really begin as soon as he or she has accepted your job offer and any conditions such as satisfactory references have been met. If you have not done so already, provide him or her with full background details about the job and your business, perhaps supplying a job description, describing the main tasks and duties, staff handbook and copies of your advertising and promotional literature, as appropriate. If he or she is moving to the area, you could also put together a local information pack consisting of a street map, addresses and telephone numbers of health centres, schools and so on, and other useful data. This need not take long for you – or one of your staff – to do and will go down well with the recruit, who may be worried about the practicalities of the move.

The induction day

You should then invite him or her to spend half or all of a day with you before work commences. Greet the employee yourself, and give him or her your undivided attention all of the time. Talk about your firm, its goods and services, customers, competitors, market-place and your plans for the future. Discuss the job, its tasks and duties, terms and conditions and all relevant rules and procedures relating to it. Also explain any odd 'terminology' in connection with your products or services, and whether you carry out some job or duty in a particular way. Make sure that he or she knows everything there is to know to avoid confusion and misunderstandings arising later on.

Show the newcomer around your premises, indicating where toilet, welfare and catering facilities are, as relevant. Point out who does what, why and where, and introduce him or her to any colleagues that he or she is likely to come into contact with on a regular or occasional basis. Perhaps they could have coffee or lunch together to get to know each other better. Afterwards, let your recruit watch his or her new colleagues at work to gain a fuller understanding of what they do, and the problems they face.

At the end of the visit, thank him or her for coming in, and check to see whether he or she has any questions or difficulties which should be addressed and resolved at this stage. Tell him or her if anything needs to be brought in on the first day, such as bank details if wages are to be paid direct to an account. Remind him or her that you are always available for help and advice on request and you are looking forward to meeting up again when he or she begins work. Make certain that he or she leaves in a positive frame of mind, eager to start the new job as soon as possible.

The first day

Before your new employee arrives for work, check to see that there is a desk and/or locker available as appropriate, and that they are clean and tidy. Remind your staff that he or she is coming in to ensure they make him or her feel welcome – it makes all the difference to a newcomer entering a well-established group. Assign his or her immediate superior or an experienced and trusted colleague to act as a 'minder' for the first day, paying special attention to and looking out for him or her, as necessary.

Meet your newcomer in person even if you will not necessarily have much day-to-day contact in normal circumstances. This will help to make him or her feel wanted, and that you are all part of the same team. Check that everything is satisfactory, before passing him or her over to your chosen minder. See him or her again at coffee-, lunch- and tea-breaks to confirm all is well, and that there are no worries or difficulties. Round off the day by speaking to him or her once more to clarify matters.

The first week

During the employee's first week at work, you should try to

speak informally to him or her at least once each day to check on developments, deal with any concerns and eliminate any problems and difficulties. As relevant, chat to his or her direct boss or the close colleague who is acting as a minder, to find out if all is well. Spot any weaknesses or shortcomings at the earliest possible stage so that they can be tackled and eliminated promptly. Perhaps make weekly checks with the employee and his or her immediate superior thereafter.

The first month

After the first month, you should make a full but informal assessment of the newcomer's progress to date. Talk to him or her, asking whether there are any problems or concerns which need to be discussed and rectified. In particular, listen out for signs of external difficulties which may be affecting work-rate and performance, and see if you can help in any way. For example, it takes time to settle into a new area, and you may be able to assist that employee and his or her family by recommending a babysitter, playgroups and nurseries, good places to eat and visit, clubs and societies and the like.

If appropriate, then discuss progress with his or her direct boss or that trusted colleague who has been acting as a minder. Find out whether they consider the employee has settled in satisfactorily, turns up on time, pays attention to appearance, works hard and well, mixes with his or her fellow workers and so on. If work-rate and performance are satisfactory, you may wish to consider confirming employment, if he or she has been employed on a trial basis.

Should you be dissatisfied with the employee, you have to decide whether or not his or her work-rate and/or performance can be improved to acceptable standards. Identify the problem, talk it through and try to discover its cause – which may simply be inexperience. This may be his or her first job, or perhaps he or she is unfamiliar with your systems and procedures. Make allowances – you may be able to just show him or her what to do, or provide training of some kind. Alternatively, you will have to consider terminating his or her employment, although hopefully this will be the last resort.

Training staff

Training plays a key role in making the most of your team. In particular, it should ensure that staff have the necessary skills, knowledge and experience required to work well, are up to date with changes and developments and are ready and able to be transferred or promoted into other and more senior jobs as and when their colleagues leave. Most employees like job training, too – viewing it as a perk, a chance to learn something new or even as a welcome break in their routine. Whatever their feelings, it keeps them satisfied and motivated, which suits you.

Training needs

To train staff properly, you must begin by identifying their training needs. These may become apparent in various ways, typically during recruitment processes, induction procedures, informal chats and discussions with employees, colleagues and their superiors and assessment interviews which may be conducted regularly to check progress. For example, an employee may come to see you with a query which indicates an underlying lack of knowledge that needs to be rectified. Alternatively, his or her immediate boss might mention that he or she is having a problem in completing a task successfully, and this must be remedied swiftly before it becomes a major difficulty.

Training requirements can be recognised in other ways too,

Training plays a key role in making the most of your team

perhaps by looking at anticipated staff changes, your future business plans and technological and external developments. As examples, knowing someone is soon to retire and must be replaced effectively, planning to produce and sell a wider product range, rapidly improving technology, and the implementation of new trade guidelines or legislation – all these suggest that training of some kind is needed for individuals or groups of employees.

Training methods

So, you have decided that an individual or a group has to be trained, perhaps to prepare him or her for another job with unfamiliar tasks and duties or for them to be able to handle new technology swiftly and efficiently. You now need to consider the best way to do it. 'On-the-job' training involves an employee watching an experienced colleague doing a particular job or activity. He or she then attempts to do the work under supervision. This trainer–trainee relationship continues on a 'watching and doing' basis, until the employee is capable of working alone.

'On-the-job' training has various pros and cons. In its favour, it is inexpensive, although you need to take account of the 'cost' of taking the trainer away from other tasks. It is easy to satisfy needs, as the trainer can go faster or slower as required. The employee will also gain practical, hands-on experience. However, you and your colleagues may not have enough skills, knowledge or time to teach staff properly, especially if the training relates to new technology which you do not really understand yourself. Also, your equipment and facilities may be inadequate for the task. Some staff may resent being taken away from other activities in order to teach their fellow employees.

'Off-the-job' training involves your staff being trained by specialists, either on your own property or elsewhere, perhaps at a nearby hotel or a purpose-built training centre. There are many organisations that provide a broad range of training courses from the government-backed, local Training and Enterprise Councils (TECs) which exist primarily for this purpose, as well as colleges of higher and further education and professional and trade representative bodies such as chambers of commerce.

This type of training offers several, key benefits, not least that courses are run by highly experienced experts, up-to-date information, equipment and facilities are available, and employees are faced with fresh and different attitudes, ideas and opinions which can be passed on to you in due course. There are drawbacks though. Courses may not match your precise requirements and will inevitably be expensive, especially when you add on the cost of travel expenses, lunch allowances and lost production. Never overlook the fact that your business may suffer when key staff are away. Also, employees are often taught too much theory on some courses, which is difficult to translate into work practice. For example, the theory of handling a dissatisfied customer in a shop can be very different from the possible reality of facing a furious and potentially violent person.

'Distance learning' is another popular training method, with staff learning about business topics via correspondence courses from organisations such as the Open College and the Open University. A package of information sheets, books and audio or video tapes may be supplied and is supported by various radio and television programmes and tutors, who are usually available by telephone for advice or by letter for marking and assessing work. Associated residential courses may be run from time to time too.

The main advantage of this approach is that it is convenient – employees can study when they want and work at their own pace. Training materials are presented in a professional and polished manner, and new information and viewpoints can benefit a traditionally run business. Nevertheless, there are disadvantages. Courses are usually costly and may sometimes be irrelevant with too much textbook theory and not enough workplace practice. As with other forms of off-the-job training, it can be difficult to translate a 'do this, say that' text into a real-life situation. Just as significant, employees have to be very self-motivated to work hard in their own time, and working alone means they cannot benefit from the immediate feedback of an on-the-spot trainer.

Training programmes

Deciding which training method to use is difficult, as many factors need to be considered. You must think about what needs to be taught. For example, a recruit who is unfamiliar with your systems and procedures should be taught on the job, whereas information about new technology or legislation may best be obtained from off-the-job training or via distance learning. Contemplate who is most qualified to teach your staff. You may feel that you would do this well, but perhaps do not have the time to do it properly. Keen and experienced colleagues or outside specialists may therefore be a wiser choice.

Consider where staff should be trained. You may possess the facilities and materials to train employees well, but are concerned that on-the-job training will disrupt fellow colleagues at work. Think how long the training will last. As an example, if it is going to be a lengthy process, it may be advisable for the employee to be trained in his or her own time via distance learning. Mull over the cost of training, including any costs such as transport, and weigh up the time spent on on-the-job training against the expense of off-the-job training or distance-learning courses.

Make your choice – which is rarely quite as easy as it sounds. If you choose on-the-job training, do ensure that you pick a trainer who wants to do it – and who is capable, experienced, and able to develop a friendly but efficient relationship with the trainee. Should you prefer off-the-job training, contact the local

Training and Enterprise Council, college or your trade representative body for advice and guidance. If distance learning is your choice, get in touch with the Open College and/or the Open University in the first instance to see what they have to offer. See 'Useful Addresses' on pages 79–82, for more details.

Training evaluation

You should always evaluate training to make sure that it has been of benefit, both to your staff and the business. Do this by talking to the employee to discover his or her views about whether it was useful, too easy or difficult, how it could be improved, if more training is required and so on. His or her opinions are important, but should be considered carefully. For example, an employee may praise an off-the-job training course because he or she enjoyed it very much, even though it might not have been of any real use. Naturally, a course should be enjoyable, but trainees must learn something relevant to their job, too.

Talk to the trainer as well, to hear what he or she has to say – whether the employee has benefited from the training, obtained new information, learned extra skills, made progress and so forth. If appropriate, check this out with the employee's immediate superior to discover if he or she can now master additional tasks and duties, and whether work-rate and performance have improved accordingly. Watch the employee at work to decide for yourself if he or she has been gaining from the training. If not, you need to find out why, and assess how you can remedy the situation, perhaps through more or different training.

Assessing employees

Larger concerns assess their staff regularly, because they believe it helps them to get the best from their employees in a variety of ways. Staff assessment – or 'appraisal' – enables you to assess an employee across a range of skills and qualities needed to do the job well and to praise and promote strengths whilst working together to remedy weaknesses. It also allows you to recognise training needs, prospective grievances and disciplinary issues and promotion prospects at the earliest opportunity. Knowing that they are being assessed on an on-going basis should keep employees on their toes too.

Naturally, you will believe – as all small business owners and managers do – that you have no time to spend on assessing staff formally. You probably have customers waiting to be served in your shop, letters to be typed and faxes to be sent, or goods to be manufactured or repaired in your workshop or factory. Nevertheless, saving time and money by not appraising staff is a false economy, as will be proved in the long term when one employee's inability to do a key task leads to an accident, another's grievance about being overlooked for promotion results in an unexpected resignation, and unchecked workers become sloppy about time-keeping, appearance and so on.

Big firms will typically assess their new staff after three, six and twelve months, and perhaps six-monthly or annually thereafter. Assessment interviews may be very formal, stiff-backed affairs, with both manager and employee dreading the interview for weeks beforehand. It need not be like this, though, especially in a small firm where everyone knows each other, mixes and gets on well together. An interview can just be an informal chat, carried out during a tea- or coffee-break, over lunch or even after work if no one is available to cover for you during the day. The important point is that you conduct an assessment, in one way or another.

Before the interview

Prior to the assessment interview, draw up a staff appraisal form. This is a document which sets out the main areas for assessment,

19

typically attendance, timekeeping, personal appearance, general conduct, work performance, work relations, strengths, weaknesses and recommendations for the future. Keep it clear and simple – you probably do not have the time to devise an elaborate one, and a straightforward one can be used for all of your employees. An example of a staff appraisal form which is suitable for small businesses is given on pages 22–3.

Speak informally to the employee about the interview and its purpose at least one week before it is due to be held, to allow him or her to gather his or her thoughts in advance. Make sure he or she is aware of its informal and relaxed nature. Hand over a copy of the form at the same time, explaining you will discuss and complete this together at the interview. If the employee's immediate superior is to attend the interview, provide him or her with another copy of the form as well.

Prepare for the interview by reading through the job description, a person specification outlining the skills, knowledge and experience of the 'ideal employee', any notes made during the employee's one-month review, and the staff assessment form itself. Think about his or her work-rate and performance. Have a chat to his or her direct boss, if relevant. Work out the topics you are going to cover, and the questions you will ask in the interview, perhaps deciding to follow the subjects referred to in the appraisal form. This need not take very long to do, and will become easier and quicker the more often you do it.

Then consider where you should hold the assessment interview, which hopefully will be somewhere quiet so you can concentrate without noise from adjacent rooms, the telephone ringing or colleagues wishing to speak to you. Make certain there are no distractions inside the interview room, such as an uncomfortable chair, bright sunlight or a cluttered desk. These apparently minor points can all affect concentration – and to be successful, both you and your employee need to be able to concentrate totally.

During the interview

Begin by putting the employee at ease – a relaxed interviewee will normally be more co-operative and revealing than a tense one. Try not to keep him or her waiting as this seems rude and increases tension. Greet the employee with a warm smile and a handshake, making polite and pleasant conversation as you walk together to the quiet room. Show him or her to a seat, and then explain the purpose of the interview again. Keep everything very low key and informal for the best results.

Step by step, work through the appraisal form together, looking at each heading in turn. Ask him or her for a self-assessment of attendance, timekeeping, personal appearance and so on. Agree on his or her strengths, and praise them. Verbal encouragement is a great motivator. Identify his or her weaknesses without making destructive criticisms. Work out how these can be eliminated or at least reduced in future, perhaps through additional training. Discuss any other problems or concerns which may be affecting work-rate and performance. For example, he or she may feel there is a lack of information given about the work that needs to be done, and communications should be improved.

Conclude the informal interview by completing the staff assessment form together in a constructive manner. Summarise the main points of the interview again, outlining the employee's strengths, weaknesses and so forth. Agree on the targets that he or she should be aiming for, and when they ought to be achieved, perhaps turning up at nine o'clock every day from now on, or increasing output by 10 per cent per week by the end of the next quarter. Decide when you will meet again. End with another warm smile and a handshake, thanking him or her for their time. Always close on a positive and upbeat note.

ASSESSMENT FORM

Name: _____

Title: _____

Date of assessment: _____

Length of employment: _____

Please tick and comment where appropriate:

	Unsatisfactory	Satisfactory	Very Good	Excellent	Comments
Attendance					
Timekeeping					
Personal appearance					
General conduct					
Work performance					
Work relations					

Please summarise your assessment of the employee:

Strengths

Weaknesses

Please recommend ways in which the employee's strengths can be developed and weaknesses can be eliminated:

Recommendations

Assessed by:	**Agreed by:**
Name: _____	Name: _____
Job title: _____	Job title: _____
Signature: _____	Signature: _____
Date: _____	Date: _____

After the interview

It is important that you follow through on the assessment interview. Do remember that staff development – in which appraisal plays a key role – needs to be a systematic and continual process if it is to be successful. Carry out any agreed measures in order to remedy or at least reduce any weaknesses. Perhaps arrange extra on-the-job training, or switch from off-the-job training to distance learning if that is advisable. Check the employee's progress towards his or her goals, and on an informal basis, encouraging him or her at every opportunity. Meet again at the arranged time to conduct the next assessment, and hopefully to congratulate the employee on his or her improved work-rate and/or performance.

Summary

- Staff development is the systematic and continual process of developing effective employees to meet the requirements of a business organisation. Induction, training and appraisal are key components of this process.
- Induction is concerned with the installation of a newcomer in a prompt and efficient manner. It can be broken down into various stages – on acceptance of a job offer, the induction day, and the first day, week and month at work.
- Training is vitally important. Staff needs must be identified, training methods assessed, programmes selected and then evaluated in due course. On-the-job training, off-the-job training and distance learning are the three leading approaches to training employees.
- Staff appraisal should be carried out regularly to spot and develop strengths, remedy weaknesses and handle problems and concerns before they become major difficulties.

3 Working Conditions

 Small business owners and managers should be aware of the need to provide a first-class working environment for their employees. This chapter considers:

- the significance of working conditions
- setting minimum standards
- making improvements
- maintaining a healthy, safe environment.

How significant are working conditions?

When the owners and managers of small firms think about getting the best from their team, most automatically recognise the importance of such areas as training staff properly, putting them into suitable and enjoyable jobs and motivating them through pay and other incentives. Unfortunately, relatively few acknowledge the underlying significance of having good working conditions.

25

Too often, this fundamental issue is overlooked or simply ignored, usually because of the time and money which would be involved in providing a decent work environment.

Yet it is important – having a healthy, safe workplace is a legal requirement, and those firms that do not adhere to minimum standards may be taken to court and fined or even closed down by a local authority or the official body known as the Health and Safety Executive (see Useful Addresses, page 81). It makes good business sense, too. Several hundred thousand employees are off work for three days or more each year due to injuries and illnesses resulting from poor working conditions – and this affects them, their families *and* you, through repair bills, compensation payments, lost production, and sometimes temporary or replacement staff.

Subject to time and financial restraints, which are always of concern to all small businesses, it is also wise to think about doing *more* than the bare minimum required to comply with the law. A pleasant working environment may be no more than a backdrop which is taken for granted, but it can help to keep staff satisfied and you can then set about motivating them through pay and complementary incentives. However, unpleasant working conditions are soon noticed and act as a demotivator. That cramped and stuffy workplace may (just) be within the law, but does absolutely nothing to encourage hard, first-rate work in a happy environment.

Setting minimum standards

Many Acts have been passed with regard to the work environment, and which set out minimum standards for all firms to abide by, regardless of their type or size. The Factories Act 1961, the Offices, Shops and Railway Premises Act 1963 and the Health and Safety Act 1974 are the leading ones in this field.

Whatever your circumstances, you need to achieve and maintain these standards to avoid the possibility of injuries and illnesses and legal action being taken against you for non-compliance. Every employer also has a legal requirement to carry out a risk assessment of the workplace to help ensure the safety of his or her employees. This doesn't have to be elaborate, and the Health and Safety Executive produces a useful leaflet – *Five Steps to Risk Assessment* – as an aid to assessment. The Employment Medical Advisory Service will also advise on your particular circumstances.

A safe workplace

Most important of all, employers must provide a safe work environment for their employees. For example, passages, stairs and floors have to be well constructed, and kept free from obstructions, unless clearly marked. Safe work systems and practices must be followed. Typically, protective clothing and safety equipment have to be given to employees when necessary, and without charge. Safety standards on plant, equipment and machinery must be upheld. As an example, potentially lethal machines have to be fenced off, checked regularly and repaired and replaced, as and when required.

A healthy environment

Just as significant as safety, employers should make certain that their premises are healthy for employees to work in. This means providing a good layout with sufficient space to work and move about in, adequate heating and ventilation, satisfactory light and noise levels and clean canteen and other welfare facilities, as relevant. Provision should also be made for accidents and emergencies which can take place from time to time, even in the safest and healthiest workplace.

**Employers must provide a safe working environment
for their employees**

First-aid facilities

Every small firm should have a well-stocked first-aid box, with staff knowing where it is and what to do during an accident or other emergency. You should also consider having at least one member of staff trained as a first-aider, depending on the number of staff and the level of hazard in the workplace. If you have any queries about first-aid provision – or any other matter to do with occupational health – contact the Employment Medical Advisory Service at your local Health and Safety Executive office. They are there to help you.

Accidents must be noted in an accident book, with details of the date, time, location, accident and injury, action taken and its consequences being written down. The Health and Safety Executive should be notified within seven days of accidents resulting in absences from work of three days or more. Immediate notification must be given for serious injuries such as loss of eyesight or limbs, death or any 'near miss' that almost resulted in a significant injury.

Health and safety policy statement

If five or more people are employed, then their employer is legally obliged to outline health and safety rules and procedures in a health and safety policy statement. This clear and straightforward document should simply set down key information such as insisting that protective clothing is always worn during dangerous processes, the procedure for checking machinery before using it and what to do when an accident occurs. The statement must be drawn up after discussions with trade union safety representatives, if relevant. It should be kept on display for all to see, or be part of the business's written rules, and should be updated when necessary. The Health and Safety Executive has produced a leaflet on writing a safety policy statement, available from any HSE Area Office.

Health and safety training

Employers must allow trade union safety officers to take paid time off to attend training courses on health and safety issues. Also, they have to set up a health and safety committee, if requested by a trade union, in order to discuss these important matters. Staff must be given enough information, training and supervision to maintain health and safety on an on-going basis. This needs to be done regularly as part of your training programme, because employees do forget what they have been told and can become careless and sloppy in their work.

Registering the firm

Those employers who own a shop, office, warehouse, hotel or restaurant must register with their local authority, whilst those which operate other types of businesses such as factories are legally obliged to register with the Health and Safety Executive. This is a relatively straightforward process which takes little time, and is in reality not much more than a formality. Do not overlook or avoid it – health and safety inspectors are more likely to help you by offering useful advice, than to hinder you with unreasonable demands or threats.

Making improvements

Knowing the minimum standards that are required in order to adhere to the Health and Safety Act 1974, you can go on to look closely at your premises to consider the improvements that need to be made to ensure you achieve these standards, will not fall foul of the law, and minimise the risks of accidents and injuries as far as possible. At the same time, think about enhancing the workplace above and beyond those minimum standards to provide an environment which positively encourages increased work-rate and performance. It need not necessarily cost a significant sum of money, if anything at all. When viewing your property, it is a good idea to study its various features in turn, putting yourself in the shoes of your employees. Negative responses suggest that improvements ought to be made.

Layout and space

To begin with, consider layout and space. Are seats and benches comfortable? Perhaps they are at an inconvenient height for using machinery. Is equipment and machinery laid out so that it can be operated comfortably? Again, some adjustment may need to be made here, to eliminate neckache and backache. Do working areas enable staff to move about easily? If not, think about making changes to them. Are all working areas safe – at all times? For example, floors, gangways and ramps must be kept clear and even, clean and non-slippery for every moment of every day. Steps, corners and obstacles must be marked clearly, with floor openings covered, or guarded when in use. It is easy to put off repairing a cracked floor immediately, or to cover a floor opening now – and sometimes such an attitude has dire consequences for employees.

Are toilets accessible and kept clean, well ventilated and in working order all of the time? Possibly, repairs are left until tomorrow when they should be done today, to reduce any risks. Are wash basins available with hot and cold running water, soap, towels and other cleaning items? Do not forget to replace soap and to clean towels often. Is there a pleasant and well-equipped area or room for staff eating and drinking? Try to provide comfortable chairs, tables, crockery, cutlery and so forth, too. Are lockers or hanging spaces available for employees' clothes? If possible, attempt to set aside a place for drying wet clothes as well. Are all areas kept scrupulously clean on an on-going basis? Typically, toilets and wash basins are cleaned, whilst a staff rest room is overlooked – which may be unpleasant and upsetting for employees.

Heating and ventilation

Is the temperature comfortable everywhere? In some workplaces, hot and cold spots exist which can be unsettling for staff. Are you able to raise and lower temperatures as required? If not, there may be times when it is too hot or cold for employees to work hard and well. For sedentary employees, such as office workers, there is a legal minimum of 16°C (60°F). Is suitable clothing provided for staff working in hot and cold temperatures? Remember that these clothes must be supplied at your expense. Is heating equipment and machinery in safe, working order? Check and service it regularly, acting *before* rather than *after* problems arise. Are all areas well ventilated? Ideally, you are looking for a plentiful supply of fresh air, but without draughts. Think about installing some form of ventilating system, if this is necessary and affordable. It could be as simple as an extractor fan.

Light and noise

Now think about light and noise to see if improvements can be made in this area. Are your premises comfortably bright for everyone? Try to have additional, local lighting for intricate and potentially dangerous processes. Are your light fittings safe? For example, you should have specially constructed fittings in flammable atmospheres, such as during paint spraying. Is there sufficient emergency lighting available in case of sudden need? If the lights go out, production may grind to a halt, unless you have made plans for such an eventuality. Are outside areas lit? This will help to make employees – especially female ones – feel safer and more secure as they come and go from the premises. Are windows and lights clean? It takes little time and effort to clean them, and staff will be happier in a brighter, fresher environment. With regard to noise, you should ask yourself these questions. Are equipment, machinery and processes quiet? If not, you should at least try to keep them as far away from employees as possible. Do machine operators wear ear plugs or muffs? Make sure that they do, and know how to fit them properly. Is a quiet refuge available for these operators between working hours? Clearly, it is not enough just to give staff tea- and lunch-breaks – they must be able to relax too. Are noisy areas, machines and processes identified with warning signs? Other employees need to be protected against noise so far as possible – so make sure they know where and when it is going to be noisy.

Equipment and machinery

Do staff know how to operate equipment and machinery safely? If not, you need to review their training again, and make sure they are instructed, trained and supervised until they do. Are safe work systems and procedures followed at all times? Staff can become careless if they are not reminded at set intervals. Perhaps more training is needed. Is protective clothing and safety equipment supplied to employees, as required? Make certain that it is up to recognised standards, is provided free of charge, and is worn and used correctly at all times. Is equipment and machinery kept in good working order? Examine and maintain it in accordance with suppliers' recommendations. Even the ordinary word processor now has its own health and safety regulations.

Accidents and emergencies

Think about your first-aid facilities, and what should be done when an accident or other emergency occurs. Is there someone who will take charge during an emergency? Ideally, there should be a trained first-aider on the premises at all times. Does everyone know what to do in an emergency? Employees should be aware of their responsibilities, such as telephoning for an ambulance, leading customers off the property, and so on. Do your emergency procedures work in practice? Spend some time practising procedures, such as fire drills. Is there a fully stocked first-aid box available? Make sure there is, that it includes basic instructions and that everybody knows where it is. Do you have an accident book, and understand how to complete it? Also be aware of your obligations to notify the Health and Safety Executive, if appropriate (see page 79).

Security

Often overlooked because there are no legal stipulations is the issue of staff protection against crime. The security of the premises against vandals and burglars can be of key concern to staff, particularly those working at night. Even during the day, staff can be vulnerable to aggression, and it is as well to be aware of this and to take precautions. On top of practical measures, such as locks and alarms, make sure the staff are aware of any common-sense security procedures and know what to do if the worst comes to the worst. Not only will this provide reassurance but it will help boost confidence in you as an employer. Do what you can in this area – and don't forget it is in your interests too.

Maintaining a healthy, safe environment

Having decided what needs to be done to meet legal requirements and to enhance the environment, carry out any improvements such as filling in a cracked floor which staff could stumble over or installing an outside security light to provide reassurance for them. It is also sensible to talk to employees about health and safety and their individual responsibilities in this field – telling them what they and their colleagues should do, and how their various duties fit together. As an example, make sure that they know who is responsible for reporting flickering fluorescent tubes, and who should replace them.

Piece together your health and safety policy statement, which is compulsory if you employ five staff or more (see page 29). Consider whether you should implement a 'no smoking' policy. Do discuss your proposed rules and procedures with employees and their union representatives before finalising this document and displaying it on a staff noticeboard – they may come up with some constructive comments and suggestions, and will certainly feel pleased to be involved in this area. Be prepared to hold regular health and safety committee meetings with employees and representatives to talk through these key issues. Of course, these meetings may be time consuming, but can also be fairly informal affairs which encourage the exchange of information, two-way communication and team spirit.

Meet and talk to these inspectors, preferably on your own property for free, hands-on advice which is relevant to your own circumstances. They will tell you more about the Health and Safety Act and other laws and explain how to interpret them in relation to your particular situation, often giving you complementary literature and being available for further, free information and advice, on request. Too often, small business owners and managers are reluctant to call in inspectors, fearing that they will find fault and then take legal action. Although this is an understandable concern – and one which all small firms share when faced with authority – it is groundless. Inspectors should be genuinely helpful and provide guidance which takes account of the time and finance available to you.

It is a good idea to learn all you can from other sources as well. In particular, your professional or trade association may offer hard, factual information and advisory material relating to your industry's needs, perhaps in the form of a code of practice. Specialist organisations such as the British Safety Council (BSC) and the Royal Society for the Prevention of Accidents (ROSPA) provide specific advice and associated materials like their monthly magazines 'Safety Management' (BSC), 'Health and Safety at Work' and 'Occupational Safety and Health' (ROSPA). See 'Useful Addresses', pages 79–82.

Whatever you do, try to keep a watchful eye on health and safety on an on-going basis – ideally, with regular, informal daily and weekly checks and more formal monthly and quarterly inspections, as appropriate. To maintain those minimum standards and hopefully to build upon them, always be on the lookout for potential hazards, accidents waiting to happen and ways of improving the environment, albeit at a reasonable cost. Keep your employees involved too – typically by making them responsible for informal checks and so on – because a loss of interest often leads to a lack of concentration and so to minor slips that can have serious implications, both for them and your firm.

Summary

- Having a healthy, safe workplace is a legal requirement and can also help to keep staff satisfied and ready to be motivated through pay and other incentives.
- Minimum health and safety standards have been established for all business premises. Employers must also carry out a risk assessment, draw up a health and safety policy statement, attend to training and register with their local authority or the Health and Safety Executive, as appropriate.
- Most business properties can be improved by studying areas such as layout and space, heating and ventilation, light and

noise, equipment and machinery, and accidents and emergencies.

- A healthy, safe environment needs to be maintained. This can be achieved by talking to experts such as the health and safety inspectors and through informal and formal inspection on a regular basis.

4   Job Enjoyment

 Owners and managers of smaller concerns need to think about the significance of job enjoyment for their employees. In this chapter, we view:

- the importance of job enjoyment
- matching employees and employment
- job improvement techniques
- redesigning jobs.

How important is job enjoyment?

At its most basic, a job may be described as 'a collection of tasks and duties', and an employee's enjoyment of his or her job will thus depend largely upon whether or not he or she is happy with the particular mix of tasks and duties allocated to that position. Naturally, each and every member of staff is different – some employees want to do easy, routine tasks without any responsibilities at all, whilst others prefer challenging, diverse tasks and are pleased to accept any additional responsibilities offered to them. Of course, there is more to a 'job' than this – factors such as work conditions, pay, working relations and future prospects are relevant, too. Nevertheless, tasks and duties are the central feature, and should therefore be considered as a separate issue.

So, how significant is an employee's enjoyment of his or her individual set of tasks and duties? Most business owners and managers would insist that it is extremely significant indeed. If a member of staff considers his or her tasks and duties to be too easy or challenging, too routine or diverse or whatever, then he or she will feel dissatisfied and demotivated, and all of the inevitable knock-on effects will follow – absences, lateness, reduced work-rate and performance, conflict, low morale, or even resignation. Thus, it is important that staff are well suited to their employment, jobs are improved as far as possible and redesigned as and when necessary – all to ensure that your employees enjoy what they do.

Matching employees and employment

When you recruited each member of your staff to date, you almost certainly adopted a thorough, step-by-step approach. Even in a small firm where time and money are limited, you should have calculated your requirements, devised job advertisements to appeal to suitable people, designed an application form to separate applicants and interviewed the leading candidates before making your final choice. Nevertheless, jobs, employees and businesses all develop as time goes by, and it is sensible to look regularly at each individual employee and their job in turn, to see if they are still as well matched as they once were. If not, changes may need to be made.

The job

Start by looking at the job in some detail. Consider its title, location and purpose. Think about who the job holder answers to, is in charge of and deals with on a regular or an occasional basis. Contemplate the main tasks involved with the job, how these are completed and the work standards that are expected. Mull over the skills, knowledge, experience and effort that are required in order to meet those standards, day in and day out.

To obtain a full and accurate understanding of the job, watch it being carried out, and even try doing it yourself to gain hands-on experience. Study your business records, such as a job description which may have been composed for recruitment purposes, and completed staff appraisal forms. Also talk to the employee, his or her colleagues, especially those in similar jobs, and the immediate superior, as relevant. Get to know each and every job really well, as if they were your own.

The employee

Working from your detailed knowledge and understanding of what the job is *now* rather than was *then*, calculate who would be the ideal type of person for the position. Consider his or her physical make up, including age, appearance, speech and health, and height and weight, too, if these are absolutely appropriate. Contemplate intelligence and attainments – education, qualifications, training, skills, knowledge and experience. Think about his or her aptitudes and interests, if these are significant. Calculate his or her disposition and any other relevant factors which you can think of which may be significant in your own particular situation.

Then take a look at the employee who is doing the job at the present time, comparing and contrasting him or her with each of the key features of the ideal person. If the job is much the same

Calculate who would be the ideal type of person for the position

as when you recruited the employee and you picked the right person on that occasion, then he or she should meet the criteria and remain well matched. However, if the work had developed or changed, or your original selection process was not as good as it might have been, then he or she will probably be ill-suited to the job and changes may have to be implemented as swiftly as possible.

The business

When you are matching employees and employment, it is important that you do not overlook the significance of your business and its changing requirements. Of course, you should know all about your existing team and their jobs in terms of ages, skills, experience, tasks, duties and the like, but remember to contemplate your proposed business developments and their effects on the types of employee and job needed in the future. You have to anticipate what will happen in advance, acting *before* rather than reacting *after* events.

Job improvement techniques

Ideally, all of your staff will be well suited to their work, good at and happy with the tasks and duties they have to perform. However, it is likely that some of your employees will be ill-matched and feel dissatisfied and demotivated – and you will need to act to remedy this situation as quickly and as efficiently as you can. One or more of three popular techniques are often adopted in an attempt to tackle and overcome such problems.

Job rotation

With this technique, staff are trained to do various jobs and are then moved regularly from one to another at agreed intervals or upon request. For example, shop workers are often taught how to manage the stockroom, serve on the shop floor, handle the paperwork in the office, and so on. They then take it in turns to adopt these varying roles. In its favour, rotation can help to relieve the boredom and frustration of having to perform the same dull and repetitive chores one after the other, day after day. Against it, employees may not do any particular job long enough to build up a satisfactory work-rate and performance. In effect, they all perform many tasks badly, rather than a few tasks well.

Job enlargement

Here, employees' jobs are expanded to incorporate the tasks and duties immediately before or just after their role in the process. As an example, in a factory, instead of having staff working on a production line with each employee completing one or two tasks in a process, every one of them is given all of the necessary parts and allowed to put together the end product. The main argument for enlargement is that it makes jobs less specialised and monotonous, but without altering the degree of difficulty involved. Opponents claim that it enables employees to complete numerous tasks, but without mastering any of them.

Job enrichment

It is often said that both job rotation and enlargement are flawed techniques because staff are doing no more than simply swapping one set of boring tasks and duties for another – and this can be true as alternative and added activities are likely to be of a similar level and nature. Typically, hotel staff may be rotated from kitchen to cleaning duties or could have their work enlarged by adding receptionist tasks to their secretarial duties, or whatever. Nonetheless, all of these jobs are evidently 'much of a muchness' – none of the employees concerned are going to be given real responsibilities or decisions to make for themselves.

With job enrichment, jobs are improved by permitting employees to tackle more complex and difficult tasks than before and to take on extra responsibilities too – at its limits, it gives them as much variety, control and responsibility for their own work as they are able to handle. The benefits of this approach are that staff are stretched, use skills and abilities which were previously unused and (hopefully) become more capable and happier employees than before. The drawbacks are that some staff may not want or be up to the challenge, and those employees around them whose jobs are not enriched, or are even reduced, can become resentful and frightened of losing their employment as a consequence of these changes.

Redesigning jobs

Having decided that one or more employees are ill-suited to their work and become aware of the key advantages and disadvantages of job rotation, enlargement and enrichment, you will almost inevitably have reached the conclusion that various jobs need to be redesigned. Certain tasks and duties can stay with the current job holders, whilst others should be reallocated amongst the remaining members of your team. Job redesign should be approached in a clear and logical manner.

The aims

If jobs are to be redesigned, it is important to identify what you want to achieve. Ideally, each revised job must enable the holder to use as many of his or her skills and abilities as possible. It should not be so simple that he or she feels it is beneath his or her competence, nor too difficult. The redesigned job must also offer variety and allow the employee to view his or her contribution to the firm as being worthwhile. He or she should have some authority to take control and make decisions, however limited they may be. It should give the job holder the opportunity to work with others as well. Whether in a shop, office or factory, everyone wants to have some degree of regular contact with other people.

The alternatives

Clearly, it is then necessary to review job rotation, job enlargement and job enrichment in turn to see which of these job improvement techniques will enable one or more of these aims to be fulfilled, in the particular circumstances. For example, job rotation may offer variety but not necessarily make the employee feel that he or she is making a more meaningful contribution to the organisation. Job enrichment might provide the opportunity to take control and make decisions, but could cause problems for the job holder trying to work with other employees.

The benefits

Hard though it may be to achieve, the probable benefits of job redesign need to be considered – they may help to keep you going through the troublesome times that lie ahead. If successful and your team feels more satisfied and motivated, then absences and lateness should be much reduced, work-rate and performance will rise leading to a higher quantity and quality of production and sales output, teamwork and morale should improve and resignations and dismissals will fall.

The drawbacks

It is equally wise to be aware of the possible drawbacks of

redesigning jobs. It can be costly – both in terms of money and time – to implement changes, especially bearing in mind the need to retrain staff and the inevitable period of resettlement when work-rate and performance may suffer. As a small firm you may not be able to afford it. Employee resistance to your proposals should not be underestimated either – however sound your proposals may appear to be in theory, it is going to be extremely difficult or even impossible to introduce them unless and until your staff are agreeable to them. Get your employees behind you.

The changes

Whatever your plans, it is sensible to consult your team before making any alterations, however minor. To implement changes without considering their thoughts and feelings may create enormous and counter-productive resentment. As an example, your initial study of a job, the ideal employee and the existing job holder may have suggested to you that he or she is overqualified for doing what you think are boring and mundane tasks, so you decide to enrich the job, by adding on harder tasks, extra responsibilities and the like. Nevertheless, he or she might be happy doing that job, and extremely unhappy about your changes.

So, talk to your employees, both those whose jobs may be revised, and their colleagues who might be affected in some way. Listen to what they have to say, and be seen to take notice of their comments, suggestions and constructive criticisms of any prospective improvements. Hear their ideas for improving their jobs, however impractical they might sound. Work through them together, agreeing on the changes that should be made, and when they will be introduced. Have the team on your side, if you want to succeed.

All developments and changes that are to be made to jobs should be implemented in a slow and methodical manner, so that staff have time to adjust and become used to them. Keep control of any changes. For example, it is easy when enriching jobs to hand over too much control to employees, giving them a free rein to vary the methods and the sequence of their work. This may suit them, but be detrimental to work-rate, performance and output. Have clearly defined standards and targets for them to work towards, and for you to check to ensure they are being met. If you have any kind of manual of procedure or code of practice, remember to update it to include any new working practices introduced.

Summary

- A job can be defined as a collection of tasks and duties. It is important that staff enjoy doing these, otherwise they may become dissatisfied and demotivated.
- It is sensible to check whether each employee is well matched to his or her employment. This can be done by studying the job, the employee and the business itself in some detail.
- Jobs can be improved in various ways – most notably through job rotation, job enlargement and job enrichment.
- Job redesign should be a slow and methodical process – identifying aims, comparing and contrasting alternative methods and contemplating benefits and drawbacks before making any changes. It is imperative to have the support of the team.

**Money is a key influence, both as a demotivating
and a motivating force**

5 Pay and Benefits

 Small business owners and managers need to think about how pay and various associated benefits can help them get the best from their staff. This chapter looks at:

- pay as a motivator
- pay levels
- pay systems·
- other financial benefits.

Are employees motivated only by pay?

Many owners and managers believe they can satisfy their staff by paying them well, and can then motivate them by handing over even more money, either through a higher hourly rate or an incentive scheme linked to production or sales. Clearly, money is a key influence, both as a demotivating *and* a motivating force. Staff may judge their value by the pay they receive and will feel disgruntled if it is not (at least approximately) in line with what could be earned in comparable employment elsewhere. Wage differences between employees must be seen to be fair and reasonable to avoid jealousy and ill-feeling arising. If employees feel comfortable about their basic pay, they can then often be made to work harder if some form of incentive system is implemented in an effective manner.

Of course, money may be a primary factor in getting the best from your staff, but it is far from being the only one. Typically, that first-class working environment and well-matched job with a sense of status and achievement should keep most employees happy, perhaps to the degree where pay is not an overriding concern, so long as it is considered to be acceptable by them. However, if staff have to labour in appalling conditions, doing boring or unsavoury jobs, then they will inevitably feel dissatisfied and only large sums of money will keep them going against the odds – and as a small business owner or manager, you will almost certainly have limited financial resources at your disposal.

So, you need to be aware that basic pay levels and pay systems that incorporate an incentive element are of significance, since they act as demotivating or motivating forces, but that there are other, equally prominent influences too. In addition to the work environment and job enjoyment, you should know about such diverse factors as discount goods and services, holidays and time off, communication and team spirit. It is important you are conscious of the ways in which they can keep employees satisfied and motivated – or dissatisfied and demotivated if they are not included in the employer–employee relationship, or such schemes are adopted in an inappropriate manner.

Pay levels

Inevitably, you will have considered and decided how much to pay when you recruited staff, and know all about how to pay them, whether by cash, cheque or bank-to-bank transfer. Also, you should have a sound working knowledge of pay administration – issuing itemised pay statements, dealing with PAYE, Statutory Sick Pay and so on. Nevertheless, it is now wise to think about pay levels again, but this time viewing them as a satisfying *and* motivating influence. In particular, how – and how far – can you use pay to encourage employees to work harder, and better?

To begin with, it is sensible to review pay levels within your firm, looking at each department (if applicable) and individual employee in turn, as appropriate. Obviously, your overall wages bill forms a major part of your total outgoings, and you will wish to keep it as low as possible so that profits are maintained at a satisfactory level. If you are paying too much in wages, you may not even make enough profit to survive, let alone grow. However, paying wages which are considered to be too low by your staff could have an equally adverse impact on your business. Not only will you find it hard to attract first-class employees, but those who are employed will feel dispirited, and unwilling to do any more than the bare minimum needed to retain employment. In all probability, they will leave as soon as they can.

Thus, when setting or revising pay levels, you need to strike a careful balance between these two extremes – paying enough to at least satisfy staff but not so much that you destabilise the firm's financial position. To help you to find the 'right' level – which naturally varies from one business to another – you need to ask and then answer a number of questions:

- *How much can the firm afford to pay out in total wages?* Clearly, you have to sit down with your accounts, profit and cash-flow projections and a calculator, and work out exactly what you can pay without affecting viability. Take account of basic pay, bonus payments and the cost of any other financial benefits such as paid time off. It all adds up. Do not pay more than your business can afford – an obvious statement perhaps, but one which many smaller firms ignore.

- *How should the money be divided between departments and individuals?* When reviewing pay, you ought to take the opportunity to consider how your organisation is structured and run, and the ways in which the wages bill is separated out amongst departments and employees. Not only will this enable you to identify gaps and overlaps in staffing levels and duties which may need to be adjusted, but you may also spot excessive differences between staff wages, and anomalies in payments to employees of similar rank or status. These can create resentment if they are not remedied promptly.

- *Are there any legal requirements concerning pay?* Here, you must take account of individual pay agreements negotiated with employees when they joined the firm, and any wage agreements made during collective bargaining with staff representative bodies. Also, you have to be aware of the Equal Pay Act 1970 whereby employees of one sex are entitled to the same pay (and terms of employment) as employees of the other sex if the work they do is the same, broadly similar or of equal value, in that a comparable degree of experience, skill and effort is required. The Act applies to large *and* small businesses and staff, regardless of their job and hours worked. The only real exception exists when you pay both male *and* female employees more money after a number of years' service.

- *How much pay needs to be given to satisfy and motivate staff?* A difficult question to answer, but one which must be addressed, nonetheless. For employees to feel satisfied, their pay may need to be similar to what they could earn elsewhere, in proportion with their colleagues' wages and reviewed regularly so that it (at least) keeps pace with inflation – so check these out. The level to motivate staff is far harder to assess and can probably only be determined through trial and error –

introducing different payment systems to see if and by how much work-rate and performance improve, and whether the business gains enough to at least cover any additional bonus payments. No easy task, especially for the small concern with limited time and resources – and none to spare!

- *What other benefits are available?* As the owner or manager of a small business, you will be well aware that pay is not – and never can be – the strongest feature of the employment package given to your staff. Frankly, many of your employees could probably make more money elsewhere in larger concerns. Therefore you – and they – have to be very conscious of all of those fringe benefits that are offered, too, and which make this a first-class firm to work for. A pleasant work environment, job enjoyment, holidays and paid time off all count as well.

Pay systems

Having reviewed pay levels within your firm, it is sensible to take a look at different pay systems and their pros and cons, especially in relation to smaller businesses. It may be that the system which you operate is not really suited to you or your employees. For example, most small concerns pay their staff by the hour, which is a simple and straightforward method but does relatively little to inspire employees to work hard and well – so, potentially, you and they lose out. Do not be reluctant to make changes if they are likely to be of mutual benefit to you and your team. Various systems ought to be considered carefully.

Payment by function

Depending on the type of work done, some of your staff may be paid an agreed salary for doing a particular job, regardless of the hours worked or their work-rate or performance. You will probably have agreed a fixed annual salary with them which is perhaps paid monthly in arrears, and in equal instalments. Occasional or regular salary reviews may take place – typically during staff appraisals – with rises being given as employees become older, more experienced and successful, or are promoted to more responsible positions or tasks.

Clearly, this type of payment system is relatively simple to administer: money due is easy to calculate and the total wages bill can be anticipated in advance, which aids budgeting and forecasting. Nevertheless, it does mean that some staff are being paid even when they are not working hard and well (or at all!), and there is no incentive for them to improve their work-rate or performance. You may need to monitor them closely and encourage them often, which is both time consuming and stressful for you.

Payment by attendance

You may pay other employees according to the number of hours actually worked, handing over payments on a weekly or monthly basis, as appropriate. In many respects, this is an ideal method for many smaller concerns – it is easy to operate, the wages owed can be deduced simply by multiplying the hours worked by the agreed hourly rate and the overall bill is known well in advance. It also appeals to the small business person's 'value for money' attitude in that they get what they pay for, no more and no less.

However, those small business owners and managers who really want to make the most of their employees will be aware that there are also drawbacks involved with this system. It cannot motivate staff to do more, or to be better. Thus, some will do as little work as they can, hiding behind their more industrious and effective colleagues. Again, you will have to watch everyone carefully and chivvy them along in order to maintain the required standards. You may soon begin to feel that you spend all day doing nothing but chasing people up, and causing ill feeling and resentment.

Payment by results

To motivate, you may wish to introduce an incentive scheme on an individual, group or company-wide basis. Typically, this may involve paying basic wages according to functions and/or attendance, with additional bonus payments linked to results. Many types of scheme exist, the vast majority of which are too complex or theoretical to be of value to smaller firms. Ideally, you will create your own, specific scheme, tied simply to the number of goods produced and/or sold. Simplicity is the key word here.

Some form of self-devised, payment-by-results scheme should offer several benefits, not least that staff will be motivated to work harder and to do better so that they take home bigger pay packets. All things being equal, an increase in goods made and sold should boost business profits accordingly, assuming there is an expanding market for them. A large group or company-wide scheme should improve staff morale and teamwork as well.

Nonetheless, disadvantages exist, too, and these need to be contemplated carefully. It is time consuming and often difficult to devise an appropriate scheme, and to calculate and check individual or group production or sales figures. Rivalry between competing individuals and groups can spill over into conflict and bitterness which disrupts departments, or even the entire firm. Quality of work may be sacrificed for quantity in the pursuit of higher wages. Also, it can be hard to work out wages bills in advance, thus making forecasting more difficult to do – and every small business needs to know what is coming in and going out at all times.

Profit sharing

This specific, payment-by-results scheme is particularly well suited to many small businesses, especially new ones which expect employees to work for relatively low wages whilst they become established in the marketplace. Applicable to all individuals and groups within a firm, bonuses are paid out perhaps on a year-end basis if or when the concern achieves certain targets, such as six-monthly or annual sales turnovers.

In its favour, such a system may help to persuade staff to stay with the company, can motivate them, improve team spirit and relationships and encourage more interest in the firm and its long-term prospects. However, some employees will feel this type of scheme is rather abstract, as there are no guarantees that bonuses will be paid in the dim and distant future. Accordingly, they may not contribute as much as others do. Should bonuses not be paid, everyone will feel unhappy and disillusioned. Even if they are, it is hard to decide who gets what, and the business could be left short of funds later on.

To decide which payment system is best for your firm, you need to ask yourself various questions. What do your staff want? Some may like stable, level pay whilst others prefer lower wages with potential to earn more. What do you want? Perhaps you are tired of chasing up hourly paid employees, but fear that large bonuses may cripple your venture. What type of system suits your firm's activities. For example, quantity of output may be more important than quality, or vice versa. Will one system suit everyone? Possibly, payment by results may be ideal for production and sales staff, but not for other, administrative employees. Can alternative systems be introduced for different departments whilst still giving a fair and acceptable deal for all? Clearly, this is a crunch question.

Perhaps you will decide to pay basic wages to keep staff satisfied and implement some form of self-devised incentive scheme which provides bonuses for success, and thus motivates employees to do better. If so, keep it simple – it should be easy for you to create, measure, check and pay, and clearly understood by your employees, who need to know what they have to do to succeed. Make sure it is acceptable to everyone. One department should not be favoured over another, nor sales staff over administrative employees. Be wary of individual or small group schemes which can generate rivalry and bitterness – try to involve everyone together.

Try to link the scheme to staff work-rate and performance only – relating it to the company's overall performance means that bonuses are subject to external pressures from the marketplace, which can be discouraging. Pay bonuses little and often. If they are paid infrequently – perhaps on an annual basis at the end of your accounting year – they appear to be rather vague, and employees may lose interest in them. Pay up promptly as well. Do not put too much emphasis on your incentive scheme, though – as a rough and ready rule, bonuses should not add more that 10–20 per cent to basic wages. Otherwise, quality will be sacrificed for quantity and an over-competitive environment will be created, with the potential for disputes. Last – but definitely not least – never pay more than you can afford!

Other financial benefits

Of course, pay is only one – albeit major – part of the overall package you can give to employees to keep them satisfied and motivated. In addition to a healthy, safe and pleasant work environment and an enjoyment of the tasks and duties they perform, there are a host of financial benefits which should be considered by you. Introducing some or all of them as rewards for long service and/or success can act as an incentive for staff and, once obtained, should make employees feel happier and more contented than before.

Discount goods and services

Nearly all firms provide their staff with cut price or subsidised products and services – indeed, many employees view them almost as an automatic right and will feel aggrieved if they do not receive them. Think about offering recruits a nominal 10 per cent discount on your goods once they have been with you for a given period, perhaps three months. Longer-serving employees can be provided with bigger discounts – possibly up to cost price – according to their length of employment. Generous discounts may help to improve staff relationships and could boost your public image too, as customers might conclude that your products must be good, if your employees buy them!

Larger businesses also have subsidised restaurants or canteens for their staff, which exist to do little more than cover costs, and keep employees feeling satisfied. The financial outlay on equipment, machinery and trained staff makes this an inviable proposition for almost all smaller firms but introducing vending machines for hot drinks and snacks, providing luncheon vouchers for discount meals at local restaurants or even negotiating cut-price deals with them may be worth consideration. Contact vending machine suppliers through your local Yellow Pages, and talk to nearby restaurateurs face to face to make appropriate arrangements.

Paid time off

Holidays and time off are always of concern to staff in any business. More often than not, they are the cause of disagreement and ill feeling, and can demotivate employees. They can be used to satisfy and motivate though, if the correct approach is taken. Even in a small venture, staff will expect reasonable paid holiday

Holidays can be used to motivate, if the correct approach is taken

entitlements according to their length of service and status. It is probably wise to operate a sliding system starting at 18 days plus public and bank holidays for trainees and junior employees, rising to perhaps 30 days for longer-serving and more senior staff. It is sensible to reward service and performance with extra, paid holidays which act as an incentive for employees to be successful, always assuming that your firm can afford to do this.

Some staff also have a *legal right* to be given reasonable, paid time off, and for a variety of reasons. Pregnant employees requiring antenatal care have this right, and it can cover any appointment made on the advice of a doctor, midwife or health visitor. The woman must have made an appointment, have asked for time off and, if asked, be able to show you proof of pregnancy and an appointment card. It may be thought churlish and a source of resentment if you ask to see these, though.

Staff under notice of redundancy are allowed by law to take paid time off to look for work or to arrange training for future employment. However, they must have worked for you for 16 hours per week for two years or for between eight and 16 hours each week for five years. Nevertheless, to retain the goodwill of your team, it is wise to permit everyone under notice of redundancy to take reasonable, paid time off to find new employment.

Should you deal with a trade union which represents your staff, its officials are entitled to paid time off to carry out union duties, if you have agreed to this, during working hours. It is up to you to decide, but will obviously do little to maintain relations and morale if you refuse reasonable requests. However, by law, you must allow union safety officers to take paid time off to receive appropriate training. This is not only a legal obligation, but makes good business sense, too – in return, they will inevitably give you assistance in maintaining a healthy and safe workplace.

Staff who perform public duties, perhaps as local councillors or justices of the peace, or who are called for jury service, are normally entitled to time off, although this need not be paid. To maintain a happy team, it is probably sensible not to stop them from carrying out their duties, unless time off becomes excessive and affects the smooth running of your business. You may also be asked to grant time off for paternity leave or on bereavement of a close friend or relative. In such situations, the amount of time off and whether it is paid or unpaid is at your discretion. It may be wise to err on the generous side in sensitive circumstances, so long as it does not adversely affect your firm to any great degree.

Sick pay schemes

Subject to various detailed rules and procedures, most staff are eligible for Statutory Sick Pay (SSP) for up to 28 weeks of sickness. There are two levels of SSP, depending on the employee's average earnings. The rates are adjusted annually, and information about this and other aspects of SSP is available from your local DSS office. SSP is paid by you to your employees, although after you have made four weeks' payments the State will start reimbursing you via the PAYE system. Clearly, your employees will suffer a noticeable and potentially disastrous drop in income during an illness if they have to rely solely on SSP – and this is distressing for those who are off sick and a nagging worry for others thinking about their future health.

To remedy or at least reduce these concerns, think about operating your own sick pay scheme, perhaps related to length of service. As a typical example, an employee with one year's service may be entitled to full pay for the first four weeks of sickness followed by half pay for the next four weeks. After that time, he or she would just be eligible for basic Statutory Sick Pay. If you pay full or half wages during a period of sickness, you will normally be entitled to a refund equal to the SSP due for that time. Of course, such a scheme can be financially costly, and will encourage some employees to take sick leave, but having a happier and more contented workforce may outweigh these considerations. It is up to you to decide.

Health insurance schemes

Some small businesses take out private health insurance for their key, managerial staff through organisations such as BUPA. Many employees will feel happier and more secure knowing they will be treated quickly and efficiently if they fall ill (although a proportion may believe that private health care is immoral, and their views should be considered and treated with respect). Prompt medical treatment for your sick and ailing staff will not only benefit them but your firm too – not least because they will be back at work sooner, fit and able to recommence work.

Similarly, it may be wise to think about taking out permanent health insurance to protect your managers against sickness or accidents which result in absences from work. If they are forced to miss work for these reasons, the insurance company will pay their wages during that period. Once again, this represents security for your most important staff, and benefits you as well since your firm will not have to pay wages for that time. To find out more about insurance schemes, contact your local insurance broker, the British Insurance Brokers Association or the Insurance Brokers Registration Council (see Useful Addresses, pages 79 and 81).

Pension arrangements

At one time or another, all members of your staff will worry about their future and what will happen to them when they retire – and these worries become more frequent and important as employees become older. Obviously, the key, overriding concern is the state pension and whether it will be substantial enough to support them – or even if it will still exist on their retirement. Accordingly, many will wish to make provision now, and you can help them to do this by establishing a company scheme which they can contribute to, or – more likely for a small firm – make arrangements for them to receive individual advice on personal pension schemes from an independent advisor. This way, you will be seen to be helpful, but without taking up too much of your time and financial resources. Contact the Society of Pension Consultants for further details (see Useful Addresses, page 82).

Financial assistance

Some businesses complete the pay package given to their staff by providing them with financial assistance as and when required. This can take many forms – most often as an advance on their wages, but also as a contribution to motor and petrol costs, payment of a railway season ticket or a subscription to a professional organisation, or a low-cost or interest-free loan, perhaps contributing towards removal or relocation expenses. Clearly, such aid can help to foster and improve relations between you and your employees, although you need to feel sure that the recipient of your generosity is a loyal employee who is not going to leave suddenly. And make certain that your firm can afford to offer this assistance. Any significant help, such as an interest-free loan, should be detailed in a written and binding legal agreement.

Summary

- Pay is a key motivator and demotivator, although it is not the only influence upon employees' work-rate and performance. Other major influences include the work environment and the job itself.

- Pay levels are important, and must be high enough to satisfy staff but not so high that they destabilise the firm's financial position. The 'right' level – which should fall somewhere between these two extremes – will vary according to individual circumstances.
- Payment by function, payment by attendance, payment by results and profit sharing all offer their own pros and cons and may suit different types of businesses depending upon their particular situation.
- Numerous other benefits such as discount goods, paid time off, sick pay, health insurance and pension schemes and financial assistance form part of the pay package given to employees. The value of these benefits should not be underestimated.

6 Employer–Employee Relations

 The owners and managers of small ventures ought to contemplate the role played by employer–employee relations in getting the best from their staff. In this final chapter, we consider:

- the relevance of relationships
- being a good leader
- communicating with each other
- building a first-rate team.

How relevant are relationships?

Evidently, the practicalities of getting the best out of your staff – staff induction and training, an acceptable pay package and the like – are important. Yet there is more to making the most of your workforce than this, especially in smaller concerns. If asked, many small-business owners, managers and employees would say that their relationship is just as significant, if not more so. A manager who takes the credit for others' work, inadequate information about what is going on around them or a lack of respect and assistance from colleagues can all have an adverse effect upon staff work-rate and performance. In essence, an ideal relationship comprises three, key factors – an owner or manager who is a good leader, two-way communication and a first-rate team.

Being a good leader

A good leader may be said to be one who fulfils his or her objectives by winning the support and commitment of his or her team and co-ordinating them to make the best use of their individual and group skills, knowledge and experience – quite an achievement! Nevertheless, it can be done, although you need to possess many qualities if you are to be successful. In particular, you must know your objectives, lead by example and be able to motivate others to follow that lead.

Knowing your objectives

To lead effectively, you need to have a full understanding of your objectives, both minor and major, and in the short, medium and long term. It is not enough to have a 'gut feeling' or an 'idea' of the direction you are taking – you must know precisely where you are going, how you intend to get there, and when you want to arrive. Your objectives – from the minor, short-term aim of clearing your in-tray today to the major, long-term one of improving sales turnover by a certain percentage over a given period – should also be consistent with each other, with all of them going in the same direction.

Armed with this comprehensive knowledge, you can make sure

that objectives are clearly stated and well understood by your team, providing each individual employee and group with agreed targets to work towards and standards to be met. Ideally, these should be challenging, so that you make the most of each person's skills and abilities, but achievable, too, as failure can be demoralising and have an adverse effect on the team. You need to be able to measure whether these targets and standards have been reached and maintained, so make them precise – to type so many letters per day, or to sell a certain number of goods per week, and so forth.

Leading by example

Of the many attributes required for successful leadership, six in particular are especially important for leading by example – self-discipline, commitment, moral courage, fairness, a caring attitude and loyalty. You must have self-discipline in all areas, such as timekeeping, attendance, dress and appearance and work practices. If you are late for work, take time off with a cold, look scruffy, fail to wear safety goggles or whatever, then your team will be equally ill-disciplined. Show commitment as well, continually striving to improve your own work-rate and performance. If you are laid back and indifferent, you cannot expect your employees to make an effort either. You may feel it is your prerogative as the owner to do what you want. Unfortunately, they will think it is their right as well.

Moral courage is an underrated virtue, but is certainly valid here. You need to be brave enough to make critical decisions and to solve difficult problems, whether to discipline staff, admit a mistake to an aggrieved employee or to make team members redundant. This attribute must go hand in hand with fairness. You have to be seen to be fair and equal in whatever you do, giving praise where and when it is due and disciplining and correcting (and consequently encouraging and hopefully congratulating) employees who deserve it.

67

There is little doubt that a good leader cares about the individual members of his or her team as people. This can be seen in many ways and should not be hard to achieve in a small, close-knit organisation – for example by knowing your employees' names, being able to talk to them about their children's GCSE's or how they enjoyed their holiday, understanding the good and bad aspects of their jobs, the difficulties they face and overcome, and so on. Loyalty is important, and hopefully breeds loyalty in return. Again, there are numerous ways of showing this – crediting their successes instead of claiming these as your own, not blaming your failures on them, being supportive in public rather than criticising them behind their backs, and so forth.

Above all, remember that your behaviour sets the tone for the whole business; and while people may choose not to follow a good example, they will invariably follow a bad one.

Motivating others

Hopefully, knowing your objectives and leading by example will help you to get the best from your staff, but it is sensible to make an added, positive effort to ensure that they do follow your lead. Set targets and standards after talks with your employees, giving them the opportunity to discuss your overall objectives, make comments and suggestions and feel involved in what they are doing. It is an obvious – yet often overlooked – fact that staff will work harder and better towards agreed goals than ones which have been imposed on them without consultation (even though these may, in reality, be one and the same).

Watch and encourage staff to progress towards their targets and standards, acknowledging their progress and congratulating them when they are successful. Genuine praise and appreciation will give them a sense of achievement and make them feel they are making a valuable contribution to the firm. Remain supportive if they fail, telling them why and where they went wrong and showing them how to improve – all without blaming or embarrassing them. Recognising their strengths and making fair, constructive criticism of their weaknesses should leave them wanting to improve, and do better next time.

Constantly evaluate and review the targets and standards that have been set, in the light of employees' subsequent work-rate and performance. With experience, you may believe it is wise to reset some or even all of these levels to bring them within reach of your staff's capabilities. Continual failure to achieve over-ambitious goals will distress and demotivate your employees. Again, have regular discussions with your workforce about this, consulting and listening to what they have to say before making any amendments or wholesale changes.

Communicating with each other

Communication between you and your staff ought to be a two-way process. You have to put across information such as instructions, advice and suggestions and should be receptive to feedback from them, whether in the form of opinions, comments or general worries. Good, two-way communication can help to scotch gossip and rumours, reduce confusion and mistrust, settle problems more quickly and efficiently and improve employer–employee relations. Many people believe that communication is the lifeblood of an employer and employee relationship, and rightly so. In a small business, most communication will be either face to face, or in writing. It is sensible to be aware of these main communication methods, how to communicate successfully and which method to choose for a specific occasion.

69

Face to face

Inevitably, you communicate with your staff on a regular, face-to-face basis – during informal chats, more formal discussions such as staff appraisal interviews, and group meetings perhaps to review sales figures. In its favour, face-to-face communication is quick and direct and allows immediate feedback with questions asked and answered, and opinions given and exchanged. It also enables you to assess how the message is being received, and to make changes in content and style as you go along. Nonetheless, there are drawbacks, too. In particular, it can be difficult to convey a complex and detailed message properly, especially if people are not listening carefully. It is literally 'in one ear and out of the other', often with no records being kept of what was said.

In writing

Your face-to-face communications with your employees will be supported and sometimes replaced by various forms of written communication. Staff handbooks will be full of information about the business, its facilities, rules, procedures and general terms and conditions of employment. Notices will convey other, up-to-date news and data about the firm and developments to the workforce. Individual and more personal messages will be passed to members of staff via memos, reports and even letters, perhaps enclosed in wage packets. A suggestion box or book may enable messages to be passed back to owners and managers from employees.

The advantages of communicating in writing are numerous. Most notably, it allows complicated messages to be passed on accurately, and without confusion or misunderstanding. Equally significant, it enables a record of the communication to be retained for further reference and verification. However, written communications may take some time to prepare in order to convey the exact message required and can be rather formal and off-putting to employees. Also, as there is no instant feedback, it is difficult to be absolutely sure whether or not the message was received and understood.

Successful communication

There are various guidelines that are broadly applicable to all forms of communication, whether an informal chat or a note placed on a strategically located noticeboard. Be well prepared – decide why you are communicating, what you want to convey and achieve. Establish your facts, and check them, considering all possible aspects, alternatives, questions and objections. Be ready to respond to queries and arguments. Think about the key areas of interest to the receiver, and any benefits to him or her. Piece together notes for a face-to-face communication, or a draft copy of a written one.

For your presentation, explain clearly why you are communicating, getting to the point as swiftly as possible. Put across your message in a relevant and logical order, staying concise at all times. Be especially careful not to repeat yourself, perhaps making the same point over and over, in slightly different ways. Use language that suits the receiver – possibly short and simple for the layperson and more complex and technical for the specialist. As relevant, mention any key areas, benefits and drawbacks of significance, working through the alternatives, objections and conclusions in turn, if appropriate. Summarise the message if necessary, just to reiterate and emphasise the main points once more at the end.

Get ready for queries, comments and arguments in a face-to-face communication whilst encouraging feedback to a written communication – usually, a response from the receiver shows interest and (hopefully) that he or she has been listening to or reading your message. Even if the response indicates a lack of attention or understanding, it gives you the chance to reinforce or correct the message. Compliment the receiver on his or her valid reaction and then work through your answer or argument on a clear, step-by-step basis. Stay polite and courteous at all times, giving the receiver the opportunity to question, check and confirm as you go along. Whatever happens, remember that two-way communication is the key to success.

The communications mix

It can be hard to decide which communication method to adopt on a particular occasion. To reach the correct decision, you should ask and then answer various questions. What is the message to be put across? Clearly, this is the first question that needs to be raised, as the contents of your message must have a significant influence on the choice of communication method. A relatively unimportant message such as a request for an employee to work through his or her lunch-break because the shop is very busy today, is best suited to an informal chat. A message about health and safety procedures, on the other hand, must by law be in writing with either a staff handbook and/or a notice being the obvious choice here.

Other questions should be considered, too. How quickly does the message have to be communicated? Obviously, face-to-face is faster than written communication. How detailed is the message? Perhaps a complex one will be confused or misunderstood if passed on verbally. How important is the message? To avoid misunderstandings you may decide to put it in writing. Is it good or bad news? An unpleasant message possibly concerning redundancy should be made face to face rather than in writing, which appears cowardly. Do records need to be kept? If they do, a group meeting with minutes being taken is better than a chat and a letter is more suitable than a note.

Just as important, who is the message for? Naturally, this is a

**It can be hard to decide which communication
method to adopt**

question that has to be asked and answered as it will have a major bearing on the communication method employed. If the message is for one person working alongside you, an informal chat may be appropriate. Should he or she be on a different shift, a memo might be preferred. If you want to communicate to a large group nearby, then a formal meeting may be most relevant, whereas a notice on a rest room noticeboard may be more applicable if the group works on another site.

Invariably, communicating with your staff will involve a mixture of both verbal and written communication methods. Ideally, a face-to-face conversation should be followed by a written communication, such as a memo, repeating and confirming the key points. Vice versa, a written communication like a staff handbook should be followed up by an informal chat or a group meeting just to ensure that it has been received, absorbed and fully understood.

Building a first-rate team

The third and final ingredient in a winning employer and employee relationship is a first-rate team, which can be defined quite simply as 'a group of people working together in order to achieve a common objective'. If you are to be successful in building a first-class team, you need to be aware of the main features of a good team and – most important of all – of key team-building techniques.

Team features

All successful teams share certain, common features. Members have a common purpose, with everyone pulling together in the same direction to complete a specific task or achieve a shared goal, perhaps to increase output or sales. They are also very aware that their team has its own identity – production line workers know their team is responsible for producing the goods, whilst members of a sales force are conscious that their team has to sell products and services for the firm. A sense of unity and belonging exists in team members.

Usually, winning teams are relatively small so that they can manage and organise themselves – dividing up tasks, sharing information, ideas and opinions, identifying and resolving problems and the like. They also have their own internal structure, with different team members assuming certain roles at given times, according to needs and abilities. They have their own code of behaviour too, to which team members adhere. A wide range of informal, unwritten 'rules' may be set, anything from going outside of the office to smoke a cigarette, to clocking each other out from the shop floor of the factory, as and when necessary.

Probably the strongest features of successful teams are that members interact with each other in order to achieve their objectives – tasks are shared out fairly, advice and guidance given, duties co-ordinated, difficulties tackled together and so on. Not surprisingly, members are very supportive of each other – typically, if one employee has an enormous quantity of work to do, the others will help, taking on some tasks and duties to ease the burden, and to make certain that the overall objectives are met, and on time.

Teambuilding techniques

Of course, it may be that your staff are already working well together as a team, although it is more likely that some developments and changes need to be made in order to improve the situation. There is much you can do to help to build a first-rate team. Make sure that you are fully familiar with the strengths and weaknesses of each individual team member, so that you can spot those areas which need to be improved, perhaps through additional training, or adjusted, possibly through job rotation, enlargement or enrichment (see Chapter 4).

Ensure that the whole team knows what its common purpose is – to maintain production, raise sales or whatever – and that everyone agrees with and accepts the objectives and the standards set. Remember to encourage your employees to participate in setting goals and expected levels of performance. Keep teams fairly small – six to eight in number, as a rough and ready rule – which should discourage cliques forming. Group together related tasks and duties that teams can organise amongst themselves, co-operating with each other to complete the work. Encourage job rotation within the team, so that members identify not only with their own tasks, but other team members' duties as well.

It is sensible to make certain that there is plenty of communication between the team, perhaps with regular, informal get-togethers to pass on facts and figures, share ideas, views and concerns, resolve problems and misunderstandings and so on. This can be done at tea-breaks and meal times. You too should play a key role in this – even though you are the owner or manager, you are still part of the team and can have a significant influence on its success or failure. Do not expect instant success, though – building a team is a slow and occasionally painful process, but given time you will succeed and be able to say that you have got the best from your employees.

Summary

- Employer–employee relations are of key relevance. The ideal relationship consists of a good leader, two-way communication and a first-rate team.

**Ensure that the whole team knows what its
common purpose is**

- A good leader knows his or her objectives, leads by example and is able to motivate his or her team to follow that example.
- Communication may be carried out on a face-to-face or written basis, but should be a two-way process if it is to be successful. Ideally, face-to-face and written communication are mixed together for best effect.
- A first-class team is a group of people working together in order to achieve a common objective. Building a winning team is a slow process, which requires time and effort.

Useful Addresses

**Advisory Conciliation and
Arbitration Service (ACAS)**
Regional offices
(Head Office)
27 Wilton Street
London
SW1X 7AZ
Telephone: 071 210 3000

**British Insurance Brokers
Association**
BIBA House
14 Bevis Marks
London
EC3A 7NT
Telephone: 071 623 9043

British Safety Council
70 Chancellors Road
London
W6 9RS
Telephone: 081 741 1231

British Standards Institution
2 Park Street
London
W1A 2BS
Telephone: 071 629 9000

**Central Office of Industrial
Tribunals**
(England and Wales)
Southgate Street
Bury St Edmunds
Suffolk
IP33 2AQ
Telephone: 0284 762300

(Scotland)
St Andrew House
141 West Nile Street
Glasgow
G1 2RU
Telephone: 041 331 1601

Chancellor Forms
Formecon Services Ltd
Gateway
Crewe
CW1 1YN
Telephone: 0270 500800

Commission for Racial Equality
Regional offices
(Head Office)
Elliot House
10–12 Allington Street
London
SW1E 5EH
Telephone: 071 828 7022

Confederation of British Industry (CBI)
Regional offices
(Head Office)
Centre Point
103 New Oxford Street
London
WC1A 1DU
Telephone: 071 379 7400

Data Protection Registrar
Whytecliff House
Water Lane
Wilmslow
Cheshire
SK9 5AX
Telephone: 0625 535711

Department of Employment
Caxton House
Tothill Street
London
SW1H 9HF
Telephone: 071 273 3000

(Scotland)
Chesser House West
502 Gorgie Road
Edinburgh
EH11 3YH
Telephone: 031 443 8731

Department of Social Security Advice Line for Employers
For basic enquiries about:
    National Insurance
    Statutory Sick Pay
    Maternity Pay
Telephone: 0800 393539
(Freephone)

Department of Trade and Industry (DTI)
Regional offices
(Head Office)
Ashdown House
123 Victoria Street
London
SW1E 6RB
Telephone: 071 215 5000

EC Information Office
8 Storey's Gate
London
SW1P 3AT
Telephone: 071 973 1992
Personal callers 10am–1pm
Telephone enquiries 2pm–5pm

Employment Medical Advisory Service
At your local Health and Safety
Executive Area Office

Employment Service
St Vincent House
30 Orange Street
London
WC2 7HT
Telephone: 071 839 5600

Equal Opportunities Commission
Regional offices
(Head Office)
Overseas House
Quay Street
Manchester
M3 3HN
Telephone: 061 833 9244

Federation of Small Businesses
Regional offices
(Head Office)
32 Orchard Road
Lytham St Annes
Lancashire
FY8 1NY
Telephone: 0253 720911

Health and Safety Executive
Area offices
(Head Office)
Baynards House
1 Chepstow Place
Westbourne Grove
London
W2 4TF
Telephone: 071 243 6000

Industrial Society
Regional offices
(Information helpline)
48 Bryanstan Square
London
W1H 7LN
Telephone: 071 262 2401

Institute of Directors
116 Pall Mall
London
SW1Y 5ED
Telephone: 071 839 1233

Institute of Personnel and Development
IPD House
Camp Road
London
SW19 4UX
Telephone: 081 946 9100

Insurance Brokers Registration Council
15 St Helens Place
London
EC3A 6DS
Telephone: 071 588 4387

Open College
St Paul's
781 Wilmslow Road
Didsbury
Manchester
M20 2RW
Telephone: 061 434 0007

Open University
Walton Hall
Milton Keynes
MK7 6AA
Telephone: 0908 274066

**Royal Society for the
Prevention of Accidents
(ROSPA)**
Regional offices
(Head Office)
Cannon House
The Priory Queensway
Birmingham
B4 6BS
Telephone: 021 200 2461

Society of Pension Consultants
Ludgate House
Ludgate Circus
London
EC4A 2AB
Telephone: 071 353 1688

The Company Information Service

Your entry to the benefits of IPD membership

As just about every element of personnel and people management
becomes more complex and demanding, more and more organisations
require professional personnel advice.

By subscribing to the Company Information Service your company will
gain access to the most comprehensive personnel management facility
in the UK. Your company will have access to our Library Information
Services and to our Legal Advisory Unit. You will receive copies of
Information Notes and Bibliographies as well as regular issues of
Personnel Management and *PM Plus*. You will receive Institute
membership discounts on a range of books, conferences and courses. In
short you will gain entry to the most sophisticated information service
available in the field of human resources and one that is normally the
exclusive territory of individual members of the Institute of Personnel
and Development.

Call 081 946 9100 for further details.